STAMPABILITY

ROSES

STEWART & SALLY WALTON

PHOTOGRAPHY BY GRAHAM RAE

LORENZ BOOKS

LONDON • NEW YORK • SYDNEY • BATH

CONTENTS

ℐNTRODUCTION

EVERY NOW AND THEN there is a breakthrough in interior decorating – something suddenly captures the imagination. Stamping is definitely one such breakthrough and it is all the more popular as it needs neither specialist knowledge nor lots of money.

All you need is a stamp and some colour and you can make a start. The idea comes from the office rubber stamp and as such it uses the same principle. You can use stamps with a stamp pad, but a small foam roller gives a better effect. The stamp can be coated with ordinary household paint – this makes stamping a fairly inexpensive option, and gives you a wide range of colours to choose from.

There are stamping projects in this book ranging from a single stamped print on a vase to a new look for your bedroom and kitchen. Each project is illustrated with clear step-by-step photographs and instructions. You are bound to progress on to your own projects once you've tried these suggestions because stamping really is easy. The added bonus is that you need very little equipment and there's hardly any clearing up to do afterwards – what could be better?

This book features three different rose designs – the large rose comes complete with stem and leaves, the small rose is more stylized and the third design shows a single rosebud. Artists and designers have always been inspired by roses. Rich colours are traditionally used in Indian and Persian textiles or French Provençal patterns. If you prefer an English country-house style, use roses in their natural colours, such as yellows and pinks, on pastel backgrounds.

Whether you use the rose stamps to make an all-over design for your walls, or just a simple border around a sheet, you'll be amazed at how effective and attractive the technique is. From now on, everything in your home will be coming up roses!

BASIC APPLICATION TECHNIQUES

Stamping is a simple and direct way of making a print. The variations, such as they are, come from the way in which the stamp is inked and the type of surface to which it is applied. The stamps used in the projects were inked with a foam roller which is easy to do and gives reliable results. Each application technique has its own character and it is a good idea to experiment and find the method and effect that you most prefer.

INKING WITH A BRUSH

The advantage of this technique is that you can see where the colour has been applied. This method is quite time-consuming, so use it for smaller projects. It is ideal for inking an intricate stamp with more than one colour.

INKING WITH A FOAM ROLLER

This is the very best method for stamping large areas, such as walls. The stamp is evenly inked and you can see where the colour has been applied. Variations in the strength of printing can be achieved by only re-inking the stamp after several printings.

INKING WITH A STAMP PAD

This is the traditional way to ink rubber stamps, which are less porous than foam stamps. The method suits small projects, particularly printing on paper. Stamp pads are more expensive to use than paint but are less messy, and will produce very crisp prints.

INKING BY DIPPING IN PAINT

Spread a thin layer of paint on to a flat plate and dip the stamp into it. This is the quickest way of stamping large decorating projects. As you cannot see how much paint the stamp is picking up, you will need to experiment.

INKING WITH FABRIC PAINT

Spread a thin layer of fabric paint on to a flat plate and dip the stamp into it. Fabric paints are quite sticky and any excess paint is more likely to be taken up in the fabric rather than to spread around the edges. Fabric paint can also be applied by brush or foam roller, and is available from specialist outlets with integral applicators.

INKING WITH SEVERAL COLOURS

A brush is the preferred option when using more than one colour on a stamp. It allows greater accuracy than a foam roller because you can see exactly where you are putting the colour. Two-colour stamping is very effective for giving a shadow effect or a decorative pattern.

DESIGNING WITH STAMPS

To design the pattern of stamps, you need to find a compromise between printing totally at random, and measuring precisely to achieve machine-printed regularity. You can use the stamp block itself to give you a means of measuring your pattern, or try strips of paper, squares of card and lengths of string. Try using a stamp pad on scrap paper to plan your design but always wash and dry the stamp before proceeding to the main event.

USING PAPER CUT-OUTS
The easiest way to plan your design is to stamp and cut out as many pattern elements as you need and use them to mark the position of your finished stamped prints.

CREATING A REPEAT PATTERN
Use a strip of paper as a measuring device for repeat patterns. Cut the strip the length of one row of the pattern. Use the stamp block to mark where each print will go, with equal spaces in between. You could mark up a vertical strip too. Position the horizontal strip against this as you print.

USING A PAPER SPACING DEVICE
This method is very simple. Decide on the distance between prints and cut a strip of paper to that size. Each time you stamp, place the strip against the edge of the previous print and line up the edge of the stamp block with the other side of the strip. Use a longer strip to measure the distance required.

CREATING AN IRREGULAR PATTERN
If your planned design doesn't fit into a regular grid, practise the pattern first on paper. Cut out paper shapes and use these to position the finished pattern. Alternatively, raise a motif above the previous one by stamping above a strip of card positioned on the baseline.

DEVISING A LARGER MOTIF
Use the stamps in groups to make up a larger design. Try stamping four together in a block, or partially overlapping an edge so that only a section of the stamp is shown. Use the stamps upside down, back to back, and rotated in different ways. Experiment on scrap paper first.

USING A PLUMBLINE
Attach a plumbline at ceiling height to hang down the wall. Hold a card square behind the plumbline so that the string cuts through two opposite corners. Mark all four points, then move the card square down. Continue in this way to make a grid for stamping a regular pattern.

Rose Cushions

Don't get your needle and thread out for this project – just buy plain cushion covers and stamp them with contrasting colours! New cushions revitalize existing decor and they can change the mood of a room in an instant. They are also a clever way to distribute a themed pattern round a room as they subtly reinforce the rosy look.

Natural fabrics like this thick cotton weave are perfect for stamping because they absorb the fabric paint easily to leave a good, sharp print. Fabric paints can be fixed with a hot iron after applying to ensure a long-lasting and hard-wearing finish.

YOU WILL NEED
backing paper (such as thin card or newspaper)
natural-fabric cushion covers in two different colours
fabric paint in white and blue
plate
foam roller
rosebud, large rose and small rose stamps
scrap paper
scissors
iron

1 Place the backing paper inside the darker cushion cover. Spread some of the white paint on to the plate and run the roller through it until it is evenly coated. Ink the rosebud stamp and make the first print in the bottom righthand corner of the cover.

2 Continue stamping in rows, using the stamp block as a spacing guide – use the top edge as the position for the bottom edge of the next print. You should be able to judge it by eye after a couple of prints. Fill the cover with a grid pattern of rosebuds.

3 For the second cover, ink all three stamps with the blue paint. Stamp each one on to the paper and cut them out. Use the paper patterns to work out the position of the rows.

4 Re-ink the large rose stamp and make the first print in the top lefthand corner. Use the paper pattern to help with the spacing and complete the row.

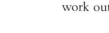

5 Ink the small rose stamp and complete the next row, again using the paper pattern for spacing.

6 Use the rosebud stamp in the same way to complete the pattern. Finally, fix the fabric paints on both covers with a hot iron following the manufacturer's instructions.

PROVENÇAL KITCHEN

This kitchen is a dazzling example of contrasting colours – the effect is almost electric. Colours opposite each other in the colour wheel give the most vibrant contrast and you could equally well experiment with a combination of blue and orange or red and green. If, however, these colours are just too vivid, then choose a gentler colour scheme with the same stamped pattern. The kitchen walls were colourwashed to give a mottled, patchy background. Put some wallpaper paste in the colourwash to make the job a lot easier – it also prevents too many streaks running down the walls. You can stamp your cupboards to co-ordinate with the walls.

YOU WILL NEED
emulsion paint in deep purple and pale yellow
wallpaper paste (made up according to the manufacturer's instructions)
paintbrush
plumbline
approx. 30 x 30cm/12 x 12in cardboard
pencil
plates
foam rollers
rosebud and small rose stamps
acrylic paint in red and green
clear matt varnish and brush

1 To make the colourwash, mix one part deep purple emulsion with one part wallpaper paste and four parts water. Make it up in multiples of six. It is best to make more than you need. Colourwash the walls. If runs occur, just pick them up with the brush and work them into the surrounding wall, aiming for a patchy, mottled effect.

2 Attach the plumbline at ceiling height, just in from the corner. Hold the cardboard square against the wall so that the string cuts through the top and bottom corners. Mark all four points with a pencil. Continue moving the square and marking points to make a grid pattern.

3 Spread some deep purple paint on to the plate and run the roller through it until it is evenly coated. Ink the stamp and print a rosebud on each pencil mark until you have covered the wall.

11

4 If you wish to create a dropped–shadow effect, clean the stamp and spread some pale yellow paint on to the plate. Ink the stamp and over-print each rosebud, moving the stamp so that it is slightly off-register.

5 Continue over-printing the rosebuds, judging by eye the position of the yellow prints.

6 For the cupboard doors, spread some green and red paint on to the plates and run the rollers through them until they are evenly coated. Ink the rose with red and the leaves with green. (If one colour mixes with the other, just wipe it off and re-ink.) Print a rose in the top lefthand corner.

7 Print the stamp horizontally and vertically to make a border along the edges of the door panel.

8 When you have printed round the whole border, leave the paint to dry. Apply a coat of varnish to protect the surface.

FLORAL LAMPSHADE

A new lampshade can work wonders, freshening up a dull corner and providing as much in the
way of style as in illumination. This paper shade has a good shape with interesting, punched edges.
However, a plain shade would work equally well for this project.
It is essential to space the rose pattern accurately, so make a quick paper pattern to ensure perfect
results every time.

YOU WILL NEED
emulsion or fabric paint in pink and green
plate
2 paintbrushes
large rose stamp
scrap paper
scissors
masking tape
plain lampshade (either paper or cloth)

1 Spread some pink and green paint
on to the plate. Ink the leaves of the
rose stamp green and the flower pink.
(If one colour mixes with the other,
just wipe it off and re-ink.)

3 Using masking tape, stick the
paper roses round the lampshade.
Make sure that they are spaced the
same distance apart and not too close
together. Depending on the size of the
shade, you should be able to fit four or
five roses round it.

4 Re-ink the stamp and lift off each
paper rose individually as you stamp
on to the lampshade itself. Hold the
lampshade firmly with your spare hand
and roll the stamp across the curved
surface to get an even print.

Two-tone Scarf

Wrap yourself in garlands of roses by stamping a silk scarf with this red and green pattern. Scarves are wonderfully versatile and they really can make an everyday outfit look very special – wear this one around your neck or as a sash, or you could even use it to wrap up your hair, gypsy-style. When you're not wearing your scarf, drape it over a chair or hang it on a peg to add dashes of colour to a room.

The scarf shown here was originally cream but it was then dipped in pink dye for an attractive two-tone effect – a light-coloured scarf would work just as well, though.

YOU WILL NEED
fabric paint in red and green
plates
foam rollers
small rose and rosebud stamps
silk scarf
backing paper (such as thin card or
newspaper)

1 Spread the red and green paint on to the plates and run the rollers through them until they are evenly coated. Ink the small rose red and its leaves and the rosebud stamp green. Stamp them on the corner and edges of the paper.

2 Slip the paper pattern under the scarf and print alternating small roses and rosebuds around the border.

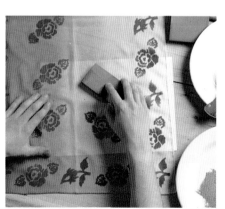

3 Fill in the middle of the scarf with two parallel rows of small roses.

BLACK ROSE VASE

The transparency of this plain glass vase creates the illusion that the black rose is floating in mid-air, somewhere above the mantlepiece. Glass is an interesting surface to stamp on because it is so smooth that the paint disperses as soon as it is applied. Have a spare piece of glass handy so that you can practise your stamp before committing yourself to the final print. This way, you can find out how much paint you need to get the desired effect.

There are now some paints available called acrylic enamels. These are suitable for use on glass and ceramics and they give a hard-wearing finish that stands up to non-abrasive washing.

YOU WILL NEED
glass vase
kitchen cloth
black acrylic enamel paint
plate
foam roller
large rose stamp
piece of glass

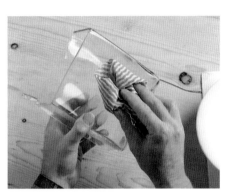

1 Wash the vase to remove any grease from the surface, then dry it thoroughly.

2 Spread some black paint on to the plate and run the roller through it until it is evenly coated. Ink the stamp and make a test print on the glass.

3 Stamp the black rose in the centre of the vase front. Apply gentle pressure with a steady hand and remove the stamp directly to avoid it sliding on the slippery surface. If you are not happy with the print, wipe it off before it begins to dry, clean the glass and try again.

TEATIME TRAY

There is something reassuringly old-fashioned about the colour scheme of this tea tray. It conjures up a picture of teas on a shady lawn with buttered slices of homemade fruit cake or scones and jam. Why not choose the colour of the tray to match your tea service and so create a harmonious look?

Any wooden tray can be re-vamped like this if you just rub back the existing paint and give it an even background colour. The green paint has been mixed with PVA glue to give it a transparent quality with a sticky texture to create a mottled print.

YOU WILL NEED
wooden tray
emulsion paint in cream and sage-green
paintbrush
PVA glue
plate
foam roller
small rose stamp
clear matt varnish and brush

1 Paint the tray with the cream emulsion paint and leave to dry. Mix one part sage-green paint to two parts PVA glue. Spread on to the plate and run the roller through it. Ink the stamp and print the top row of roses with the leaves all facing the same direction. Print the bottom row with the leaves facing the opposite direction.

2 Fill in the middle rows of roses as shown, then stamp around the inside of the tray sides.

3 Use the roller to paint the top of the tray sides with a solid stripe of sage-green paint.

4 When dry, apply at least two coats of clear matt varnish. A tinted varnish will give an aged appearance.

COTTAGE BEDROOM

Stamp denim-blue roses on to an off-white background and decorate bed linen to match. If your walls are pristine and smooth, there are ways to create the effect of rough plaster. It may seem perverse to roughen up a nice, smooth wall, but there is nothing to compare with the character imparted by irregular plasterwork. The trick here is to scratch the walls to provide a "key" to work on and then to apply a coat of filler, varying the depths in places. Leave this to set, then rub some of it away before it has completely hardened – this will give a deep distressed look. Use a rasp and coarse sandpaper to roughen up the rest of the wall, and you will have created your own cottage walls.

YOU WILL NEED
emulsion paint in white, buttermilk-yellow
and denim-blue
large paintbrush
plumbline
approx. 30 x 30cm/12 x 12in cardboard
pencil
plate
foam roller
large rose, rosebud and small
rose stamps
royal blue fabric paint
scrap paper
scissors
plain white sheets
iron
backing paper (such as thin card or
newspaper)

1 Paint the walls white, then make a colourwash by mixing four parts water to one part buttermilk-yellow. Brush this on to the walls, using random, sweeping strokes. If runs occur, just pick them up with the brush and work them into the surrounding wall.

2 Attach the plumbline at ceiling height, just in from the corner. Hold the cardboard square against the wall so that the string cuts through the top and bottom corners. Mark all four points with a pencil. Continue moving the square and marking the points to make a grid pattern.

3 Spread some denim-blue paint on to the plate and run the roller through it until it is evenly coated. Ink the large rose stamp and print one rose on every pencil mark.

4 Ink the rosebud stamp and print between the large roses to complete the pattern.

5 For the sheets, spread some royal-blue paint on to the plate and run the roller through it until it is evenly coated. Ink the small rose stamp and make prints on the paper. They will be used to work out the spacing.

6 Cut out the rose prints from the paper. If you do not have enough to work out a complete pattern across the sheet, print some more.

7 Wash and iron the sheet prior to stamping to ensure the best prints.

8 Place the backing paper under the ironed sheet.

9 Position the paper cut-outs on the sheet, rearranging them until you are happy with the design. You could make an all-over pattern of staggered rows, or simply print a border along the top.

10 Ink the stamp with the roller, and print the roses, using the paper cut-outs as a guide. If you are printing a border, line up the sewn border edge against the top of the stamp block to keep the line straight.

11 Fix the fabric paint with a hot iron following the manufacturer's instructions.

PATTERNED FLOORCLOTH

Here is an unusual alternative to buying an expensive runner-rug – simply make a floorcloth out of plain artist's canvas.

Floorcloths were originally used by American settlers who found that sailcloth could be stretched over a bed of straw to cover their hard floors. They decorated them to imitate checkered marble floors and fine carpets, and found that the paint and varnish added to their durability. They were eventually replaced by the invention of linoleum, but have recently come back into fashion.

Artist's canvas comes in many widths – just think of the paintings you've seen – and it is available through arts and crafts suppliers.

YOU WILL NEED
plain cream artist's canvas (cut to size)
pencil
ruler
scissors
fabric glue and brush
white acrylic primer
paintbrush
black emulsion paint
plate
foam roller
rosebud, small rose and large rose stamps
scrap paper

2 Spread some black paint on to the plate and run the roller through it until it is evenly coated. Ink all the stamps and print a circular repeat pattern on to the paper. You could use a plate to help draw an accurate circle.

3 Stamp six small roses along the bottom edge of the floorcloth.

1 Draw a 4cm/1½in border around the edge of the canvas, then fold this back to make a seam. Mitre the corners by cutting across them at a 45-degree angle, then apply the glue and stick the seams down flat. Turn the canvas over and apply one or two coats of white acrylic primer.

4 Place the paper pattern over the floorcloth and lift it up as you stamp each element of the pattern on to the cloth. After you have printed the first circle pattern, you will get to know the order of the prints, and you may not need to refer to the paper pattern so often.

5 Leave the first completed circle to dry thoroughly before placing the paper pattern on to the next section and stamping the pattern as before. When you have repeated the pattern along the length, finish off the top edge of the floorcloth with the same six small roses that you started with.

ROSE LIVING ROOM

New homes are wonderfully fresh, but the perfectly-even walls can look plain if you are used to details such as dado-rails and deep skirting boards. This project shows you how to retain the freshness of new pastel paintwork and add interest with a frieze at dado-rail height and a coat of colourwash below it.

Don't worry about painting in a straight line for the frieze – just use two strips of low-tack masking tape and paint between them. You could even try doing it by hand, as it does add character to the decoration, even if you do wobble a bit!

Wooden furniture is given a distressed paint finish in toning colours, and stamped with the rose designs to co-ordinate with the walls.

YOU WILL NEED
sandpaper (optional)
emulsion paint in cream, blue-green,
dusky-blue and peach
paintbrush
cloth
plates
foam roller
scrap paper
rosebud, small rose and large rose stamps
tape measure
pencil
wallpaper paste (made up according to the
manufacturer's instructions)
masking tape
spirit level
straight-edged plank of wood
square-tipped 2.5cm/1in artist's brush

2 Spread the dusky-blue paint on to the plate and run the roller through it. Ink the rosebud stamp and print the design on to the paper.

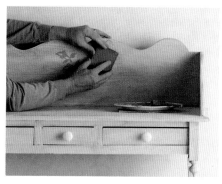

3 Referring to the paper pattern, stamp the design in position on your chosen piece of furniture.

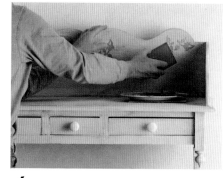

1 To prepare the furniture, rub each piece down with sandpaper and apply a coat of cream paint. Make the blue-green glaze by diluting one part paint with three parts water and then brush it on following the direction of the grain. Before the paint has dried, use a cloth to wipe off some of the paint.

4 Stamp more rosebuds on either side of the central design. Work with the shape of the furniture to decide upon the best position and the number of prints.

5 If you are decorating a desk or dresser, unscrew and remove any handles, then stamp the pattern on the drawer fronts. Screw them back after the paint has dried.

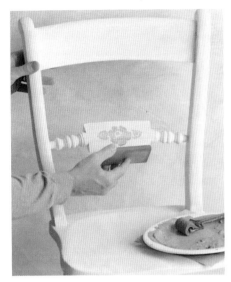

6 For a small piece of furniture like this chair, a simple design is best. Paint the chair cream, then print a single small rose in peach.

7 To make the colourwash for the walls, mix one part peach emulsion paint with one part wallpaper paste and four parts water. Make it up in multiples of six. It is best to make more than you need, so that you can do the whole room from the same batch to ensure a colour match.

Unless the room has been painted recently, apply a coat of cream emulsion to the walls.

8 Measure about 90cm/36in from the floor and make a pencil mark on the wall. Tape the spirit level to the plank and draw a straight line all round the room 90cm/36in above floor level. Draw another line 3cm/1¼in above it.

9 Apply the colourwash below the line using sweeping random brushstrokes. If runs occur, just pick them up with the brush and work them into the surrounding wall. Aim for a patchy, mottled effect.

10 If you have a steady hand, paint the dusky-blue stripe with the square-tipped brush, otherwise use masking tape to guide you and remove it when dry.

11 Spread the dusky-blue and peach paints on to the plates and use the foam roller or paintbrush to ink the large rose stamp, using the colours as shown. Print with the stamp base resting on the top of the blue stripe. Continue all round the room, re-inking each time for a regular print.

Tumbling Rose Chair Cover

Ready-made slip covers for director's and wicker chairs provide an innovative way of restyling a room. It is rather like putting on a new jacket and changing your image.

The design of the roses follows the curve of the chair and the direction of the seat. One of the advantages of these covers, is that you can use them to disguise less than perfect chairs that are still structurally sound. Look out for old Lloyd loom chairs with sprung seats – their appearance may have been spoiled by coats of gloss paint over the years, but they're still ideal for a slip cover.

YOU WILL NEED
fabric paint in green and red
plate
foam rollers
large rose stamp
ready-made calico slip cover
backing paper (such as thin card or newspaper)
iron

1 Spread some green and red paint on to the plate and run the rollers through them until they are evenly coated. Ink the rose red and the stalk and leaves green.

2 Place the backing paper behind the front panel of the slip cover and begin stamping the roses. Rotate the stamp in your hand after each print to get the tumbling rose effect.

3 Place the backing paper behind the seat section and stamp the roses in the same way as the front.

4 Place the backing sheet inside the top section and stamp the top row, following the shape of the slip cover. Continue stamping to fill the cover, rotating the stamp as you did before. Fix the fabric paint on the chair cover with a hot iron following the manufacturer's instructions.

First published in 1996 by Lorenz Books

Lorenz Books is an imprint of Anness Publishing Limited
Boundary Row Studios
1 Boundary Row
London SE1 8II IP

ISBN 1 85967 245 0

Distributed in Canada by Raincoast Books Limited

A CIP catalogue record for this book is available from the British Library

Publisher: Joanna Lorenz
Senior Editor: Lindsay Porter
Assistant Editor: Sarah Ainley
Designer: Bobbie Colgate Stone
Photographer: Graham Rae
Stylist: Diana Civil

Printed and bound in Singapore

ACKNOWLEDGEMENTS
The authors and publishers would like to thank Sacha Cohen and Ron Barber for all their hard work in the studio.

Paints suplied by
Crown Paints, Crown Decorative Products Ltd, PO Box 37, Crown House, Hollins Road, Darwen, Lancashire, BB30 B6
Specialist paints supplied by Paint Magic, 79 Shepperton Road, Islington, London N1 3DF